T0099934

Journal Bites

It's *Standard* to write during reading.

Reproducible Standards-based prompts for
combining writing and reading
across the curriculum

Literary Response
Science
Social Studies

Sonia Tuttle & Kathleen Haley

authorHOUSE®

AuthorHouse™
1663 Liberty Drive
Bloomington, IN 47403
www.authorhouse.com
Phone: 1-800-839-8640

First published by AuthorHouse   5/11/2009

ISBN: 978-1-4389-6055-5 (sc)

Printed in the United States of America
Bloomington, Indiana

This book is printed on acid-free paper.

PREFACE

As a writing coach, I have heard countless times that there is not enough time to teach writing. Understanding that teaching writing does not have to be a lesson separate from other subject areas, would change the way teachers look at teaching students. To be meaningful, writing should be included in all areas of the curriculum. *It should be considered to be the way we communicate what we know or what we have learned.*

When children write, they don't have the same experiences as adults. Therefore, when assigning a writing lesson, teachers cannot simply give them a statement and ask them to write about it. We must give them some support for how to get their limited ideas onto paper. The writing prompts in this book contain questions to get students thinking about what they know.

Journal writing is a great way to get your students writing every day. Short writing lessons can be done when students enter classrooms in the morning, later in the day for reflection on something read, or as hooks for lessons. Discussing what students have written, and having them share their writing with others, are not activities that are meant to be graded. They are meant to be a higher level of communication than simply answering questions on a worksheet.

The journal prompts in this book will give you ideas for getting started. They can be copied and used as they are or as examples for writing meaningful prompts based on what is being studied. By using the prompt format in this book, you will be able to write prompts that will result in longer, more organized student writing. Many of the questions in these prompts are based on permanent memory research. *For lessons that help students retain information in permanent memory, they must involve repetition, deep processing, and making connections to what they know or have learned.*

TABLE OF CONTENTS

INTRODUCTION

In my experience as a writing coach, I have seen teachers struggle with teaching writing. Many teachers treat writing as an isolated subject and claim that there is no time in the day for formal writing instruction. Getting well-written prompts into the hands of teachers is crucial for teaching writing.

Students should be challenged with meaningful strategies in a way that draws on what is being studied and on background knowledge. For students to gain meaning from writing, they must be able to draw on what they have learned, and apply their knowledge of the writing process. Students are expected to write regularly, but are not provided with the instruction needed to build on prior knowledge or long-term memory. For this reason, it is important to write daily about topics being studied and then take time to process, discuss, and share information they have learned from the writing.

Journal prompts are an ideal way to enhance writing and long-term memory because they can be done quickly and for different purposes. In this way, students will come to understand that writing is a way of communicating rather than simply another subject in their school day.

Note: Before giving a journal prompt to students, it is important for teachers to read the prompt and write a response. Doing this will provide teachers with an insight into any difficulty students might have in understanding what they are expected to do as well as the variety of answers that are possible for later discussion. The teacher's response can be used to initiate discussion with students and to show how all responses will not and should not be the same.

LITERARY RESPONSE

Students in all grades are expected to write in response to reading. These responses can and should be done in all subject areas. In State Standards, this is known as Literary Response.   Indicators in Literary Response include the following skills:

- *Comparing and/or contrasting two characters, stories, plots, settings, etc.*

- *Retelling a story*

- *Creating different endings for stories*

- *Comparing stories from different cultures*

- *Responding to or comparing different genres*

- *Writing about the theme*

- *Responding to the vocabulary in writing, such as alliteration, figurative language, etc.*

- *Writing about causes and effects found in stories*

- *Responding to a character's actions*

- *Writing about conflicts and resolutions*

- *Evaluating patterns and symbols found in literature*

- *Analyzing the influence of the setting on problems and resolutions*

- *Responding to fantasy and reality situations*

On the following pages, you will find journal prompts that will address these standards and indicators.

Journal Prompt

Literary Response

Choose two characters from the story.

- Compare the characters by telling how they are alike.
- Tell how the characters are different.
- Tell which character is most like you, and why.

Journal Prompt

Literary Response

Stories often have more than one main character.

- Choose one main character and describe him or her.
- What problem did the character face in the story?
- How did the character resolve the problem?

JOURNAL PROMPT

Literary Response

Think about the story you just read. In this story, the character's appearance was important to the plot.

- Describe the character's appearance.
- How does the character's appearance affect the plot?

JOURNAL PROMPT

Literary Response

Sometimes characters in a story learn a lesson that makes their actions change in some way.

- How did the character's actions change in this story?
- What caused the change?
- Tell about something that has happened to you that has caused you to change your actions.

JOURNAL PROMPT

Literary Response

Choose a character in the story (or reading passage.)

- Explain how the character's actions helped you understand the character.
- Tell if you agree or disagree with the character's actions.
- Describe how you are like or not like this character.

JOURNAL PROMPT

Literary Response

Settings often change during a story.

- Describe two different settings in the story.
- Explain why settings change.
- Tell if either of these settings reminds you of a place you have been. If so, where was it?

JOURNAL PROMPT

Literary Response

Think about the story you just read.

- What influence did the setting have on the problem in the story?
- Did the setting influence the resolution of the problem? In what way?
- Describe a setting that would have had a different influence on the problem and resolution.

JOURNAL PROMPT

Literary Response

Think about the story you have just read.

- How did the fact that the character is in a familiar setting affect the action in the story?
- What would be different if the setting were not familiar to the character?
- How do you feel when you're in an unfamiliar setting?

JOURNAL PROMPT

Literary Response

Think of an important event that has happened in your life.

- Make an organizer showing the causes and effects of this event.
- Explain how the effects of this event did or did not change your life.
- What did you learn from this event in your life?

JOURNAL PROMPT

Literary Response

Look at this picture.

What do you think this picture is trying to tell you?

JOURNAL PROMPT

Literary Response

Sometimes authors surprise us with the ending they choose for a story.

- Describe how the story ended.
- Rewrite the ending choosing one of the following: *happy, sad, funny.*
- How is the ending important to the story?

JOURNAL PROMPT

Literary Response

Think about the story you are reading.

- Predict what will happen next.
- Why do you think this?
- Think about another way this story could end. What is it?

JOURNAL PROMPT

Literary Response

In the story there were several conflicts. Choose one.

- Describe the conflict.
- Explain how the conflict was resolved in the story.
- Tell if you have ever been faced with this conflict.

JOURNAL PROMPT

Literary Response

The country and the city have many similarities and differences.

- Compare living in the country to living in the city.
- In which place would you rather live and why?

JOURNAL PROMPT

Literary Response

Everyone is unique in some way.

- What made the main character in the story unique?
- Compare yourself to the main character in the story.
- Do you think it is important to be unique? Why?

JOURNAL PROMPT

Literary Response

There are many different kinds of sports, such as football, skateboarding, and volleyball. Each sport has athletes who perform well in that sport. An example would be: Peyton Manning is an athlete who plays football.

- Choose two athletes from the same sport and compare them.
- How are you like one or both of these athletes?

JOURNAL PROMPT

Literary Response

The main idea an author wants the reader to understand is called "theme."

- What is the theme of this story?
- What other story have you read with the same or a similar theme?
- How does this theme relate to your life?

JOURNAL PROMPT

Literary Response

Think about the story you are reading.

- What is the theme?
- How did the author support this theme in the story?

JOURNAL PROMPT

Literary Response

Think about the passage you are reading.

- What is the story mostly about?
- List some details from the story that support this main idea.
- How important is this topic to you and your life? Why?

JOURNAL PROMPT

Literary Response

Think about the story (or passage) you just read.

- Explain how you know the story is fantasy or reality.
- Give some examples from the story.
- Does a story have to be all fantasy or all reality? Explain your answer.

JOURNAL PROMPT

Literary Response

Think about the passage you have been reading.

- Find an example of a fact in the text.
- Find an example of an opinion.
- How did you know the difference?

JOURNAL PROMPT

Literary Response

You have been reading stories from different cultures.

- Give an example of how the cultures were different.
- Which culture is most like yours, and why?
- Do you think it is important to read about other cultures? Why?

JOURNAL PROMPT

Literary Response

Think about the way you look. Describe your external features.

- When people look at you, what features do they see?
- Draw a picture of these features.

JOURNAL PROMPT

Literary Response

Some animals have common traits, but are also different in some ways. One example of this is a dog and a cat.

- How are dogs and cats alike?
- How are they different?
- Which would make a better pet? Why?

Journal Prompt

Literary Response

Construct a time line to show the events in the passage in chronological order.

Journal Prompt

Literary Response

Many people like to travel. Think of a place that you would like to visit.

- Describe what you would see, hear, taste and smell.
- Tell how you would feel if you were in this place.
- List some items needed for your trip *in order of importance.*

NARRATIVE

We often ask students to write stories. When they attempt to write from their own experiences and prior knowledge in a fictional way, they are writing narratives. In these stories, we should be able to hear the voice of the student. The following is an example of a narrative prompt.

Write about what you would do if you could spend a day any way you wanted.

- *What would you do?*
- *Who would you see?*
- *Where would you go?*

JOURNAL PROMPT

Narrative

You hear the radio announcer say there will be no school today due to a foot of snow falling the night before.

- Describe what you see when you look out your window.
- Explain what you will do on this day.
- Tell whether you think snow days are good or bad, and why.

JOURNAL PROMPT

Narrative

Dr. Martin Luther King, Jr. Day is celebrated in January.

- Tell why we celebrate Dr. Martin Luther King, Jr.
- Explain how Dr. King has affected your life in some way.
- Tell how you think Dr. King would feel about this holiday.

Journal Prompt

Narrative

In the winter students often have to stay inside for recess.

- Give some reasons for staying inside.
- Tell what your class does during inside recess.
- Explain how you feel about recess being inside.

Journal Prompt

Narrative

People often move away from home as they get older. Sometimes they move far away.

- Give some reasons why people might move far away from their home.
- If you could move away, where would you choose to go? Why?
- Would you want to visit this place before you made your decision? Explain your answer.

PERSUASIVE

Persuasive prompts are meant to be used when arguing for or against an issue. It is important to be able to defend an argument, using examples and reasons for your decision. The following is an example of a persuasive prompt.

Your school has decided that all busses will play classical music on the rides to and from school.

- *Do you agree or disagree with your school's decision?*
- *In what ways might this be a good decision?*
- *In what ways could this be a bad decision?*

JOURNAL PROMPT

Persuasive

In the winter students often have to stay inside for recess. Your teacher thinks it might be best to cancel indoor recess.

- What reasons could you give for keeping indoor recess?
- When might it not be a good idea?
- How else could this time be spent?

JOURNAL PROMPT

Persuasive

Your teacher has told you that there will no longer be field trips for students.

- How does this make you feel?
- How do field trips help students learn?
- If you were given a chance to persuade your teacher to let you go on one more field trip, where would you ask to go? Why?

JOURNAL PROMPT

Persuasive

Your favorite singer or singing group has just arrived in town. You want to go to the concert, but your parents can't decide if you should go.

- Describe your favorite singer or singing group.
- Explain when and where the concert will take place.
- Explain to your parents why they should let you go.

JOURNAL PROMPT

Persuasive

Your school has decided that everyone will wear uniforms.

- Describe the uniforms.
- Explain why your school has made this decision.
- Argue for or against this decision.

Figurative Language

Authors often use literary devices such as figurative language to make their writing more interesting. Figurative language helps to paint pictures in the minds of readers to help them remember what is read. The following examples of figurative language are included in Literary Response in State Standards.

- Simile: a comparison that uses like or as
                   The stars sparkled like diamonds in the night sky.

- Metaphor: an implied comparison
                   The stars were diamonds in the night sky.

- Hyperbole: an exaggeration for effect
                   The sheets hanging on the line were whiter than white.

- Personification: a description that represents a thing as a person
                   The rabbit checked his watch as he ran by.

- Symbolism: the use of an object to represent something else
                   Pictures of donkeys and elephants were hung around
                   the room, reminding us to vote on Tuesday.

- Imagery: the use of language to create vivid pictures in the
                   reader's mind
                   The setting sun poured a syrupy darkness over the forest.

- Idiom: an expression that cannot be figured out based on the literal
                   meaning of the words in the expression
                   The questions on the test were over the girl's head.

JOURNAL PROMPT

Figurative Language

Authors use similes and metaphors to make comparisons in stories.

Metaphor example*:* *The sun was a huge red ball in the summer sky.*
Simile example*:* *The stars twinkled like diamonds.*

- Write an example of a simile or metaphor.
- Explain why authors might use these types of figurative language when writing.

JOURNAL PROMPT

Figurative Language

Read the two sentences below. The first one is a simile and the second is a metaphor.

The stars were like diamonds in the night sky.
The stars were diamonds in the night sky.

- How is a simile different than a metaphor?
- Why do you think writers use these types of figurative language in their writing?
- Write either a simile or a metaphor to describe something in your life.

Sonia Tuttle -Journal Bites- 2009

JOURNAL PROMPT

Figurative Language

Idioms are often used by authors to say something in a different way. "Raining cats and dogs" is an example of an idiom.

⇒ Draw pictures to show the literal and figurative meanings of "raining cats and dogs."

Literal Meaning
(What is said)

Figurative Meaning
(What the author really means)

JOURNAL PROMPT
Figurative Language

Crying "crocodile tears" is an idiom meaning to pretend to be sad about something when you are really not. Think of a time when you cried crocodile tears.

- When was it?
- Was this a good idea or a bad idea? Why?

JOURNAL PROMPT

Figurative Language

Authors often use imagery to make their writing more descriptive.

- Give an example of imagery from the passage.
- Why do you think authors use this technique in their writing?
- Use imagery to describe something in your life.

JOURNAL PROMPT

Figurative Language

In this story, the author uses figurative language. Find an example in the story.

- What type of figurative language did the author use?
- Do you think the use of figurative language makes the reading more interesting? Why?
- Write an example of your own using the same technique the author used.

GENRE

Students are expected to identify and understand differences in various genres when responding to literature. The following genres are included when being asked to perform these tasks.

◊ *Fiction*
◊ *Nonfiction*
◊ *Biographies*
◊ *Autobiographies*
◊ *Poetry*
◊ *Fairy Tales*
◊ *Fables*
◊ *Myths*
◊ *Legends*
◊ *Fantasies*

JOURNAL PROMPT

Genre

Fiction and nonfiction are different genres, or forms of writing.

- Compare the organization of the two genres.
- Which genre makes it easier to go back and find information?
- Which genre do you like best? Why?

JOURNAL PROMPT

Genre

A biography is a story that is written about someone's life by someone other than that person. Think about some biographies you have read.

- What is one biography you have read?
- How are biographies different from other books?
- If you had to write a biography about someone's life, who would you choose? Why?

JOURNAL PROMPT

Genre

Poetry is written differently than other genres, or forms of writing.

- What are some characteristics of poetry?
- Choose one of these characteristics and explain how authors use it to make a point.
- Explain how you feel about reading poetry.

JOURNAL PROMPT

Genre

Legends are a genre of writing that is used for explaining how something came to be. Native Americans told many stories explaining why things are the way they are, such as why a particular flower looks the way it does.

- Why do you think people living long ago created legends to explain things?
- Do you think these stories are still told today exactly as they were long ago? Why or why not?
- If you were asked to create a legend to explain something in nature, what would you choose to explain?

REFERENCE TOOLS

Students are expected to know how to use reference materials. These materials include the following.

◊ *Thesaurus*
◊ *Dictionary*
◊ *Atlas*
◊ *Internet*

Asking students to write about these materials can be necessary for understanding when and why to use them.

JOURNAL PROMPT

Reference Tools

Using a thesaurus can help you when writing.

- When would it be helpful to use a thesaurus?
- How could this help make your writing better?

JOURNAL PROMPT

Reference Tools

A thesaurus is a book of synonyms and antonyms.

- In what way would a thesaurus be helpful when writing?
- Writers spend a lot of time trying to choose the correct words when writing. Why do you think they do this?

JOURNAL PROMPT

Reference Tools

Dictionaries are useful resources.

- For what reasons would you use a dictionary?
- If you did not have a dictionary, where else could you find this information?

JOURNAL PROMPT

Reference Tools

Students are often asked to write words in alphabetical order.

- Is this hard for you to do? Why?
- When might you need to know how to alphabetize words in your daily life?

JOURNAL PROMPT

Reference Tools

Reference materials can be used for various purposes.

- Do you think an atlas is a useful reference material? Why?
- When might you use an atlas in your life?

JOURNAL PROMPT

Reference Tools

The internet is a great tool for finding information.

- When might it be useful to use the internet?
- How do you use the internet?
- How did people find information before the internet existed?

SOCIAL STUDIES

Writing in response to reading should take place in all subject areas. In Social Studies students can respond using the same skills mentioned in Literary Response. Students are responding to informative or expository text.

JOURNAL PROMPT

Social Studies

Our world is made up of many different cultures. One thing that can be different from one culture to another is food.

- Choose one culture that you have been reading about. What is it?
- What foods are important to this group of people?
- Do you eat some of these foods in your culture? Explain your answer.

JOURNAL PROMPT

Social Studies

Our world is made up of many different cultures. Each cultural group may dress a little differently.

- Choose a cultural group from your reading.
- How do the people in this cultural group dress?
- How is this similar to or different from the way you dress in your culture?

Journal Prompt

Social Studies

Every culture has certain traditions and customs that they follow on holidays.

- Choose one cultural group and an important holiday in this culture.
- What traditions are shared by this group during this holiday?
- How are these traditions similar to or different from the way your family celebrates this holiday?

Journal Prompt

Social Studies

Freedom is a wonderful thing. In the United States we have many freedoms.

- What is one freedom we have in the United States?
- Do all countries share this freedom?
- Why do you think we have more freedoms than some countries?

JOURNAL PROMPT

Social Studies

The Statue of Liberty is a symbol of freedom in the United States. The following is from the New Colossus by Emma Lazarus and can be seen on the pedestal of the Statue of Liberty.

> *Give me your tired, your poor,*
> *Your huddled masses yearning to breathe free,*
> *The wretched refuse of your teeming shore.*
> *Send these, the homeless, tempest-tost to me,*
> *I lift my lamp beside the golden door!*

- What do you think these words mean?
- What words in the passage helped you understand the meaning?
- Are there words you do not understand? What are they?

Journal Prompt

Social Studies

The following are symbols of the United States.

Uncle Sam   *Bald Eagle*
Liberty Bell   *Statue of Liberty*

- Choose one of these symbols and explain why you think it represents the United States.
- If you could choose a **new** symbol to represent the United States to people from other countries, what would you choose and why?

Journal Prompt

Social Studies

Artifacts used by human beings who lived long ago have been found by archaeologists.

- What are artifacts?
- How do we know something is an artifact?
- What can we learn from artifacts?

JOURNAL PROMPT

Social Studies

Artifacts have been found that show evidence of the possible behavior of human beings who lived long ago.

- Describe an artifact that could show a behavior of a group of people.
- What artifacts from your life might people find a thousand years from now?
- What would these artifacts tell someone about you?

JOURNAL PROMPT

Social Studies

Immigrants are people who move from one country to another. The United States has immigrants from countries all over the world.

- Why might people want to come to the United States to live?
- Do you think this is a good thing or a bad thing? Why?

JOURNAL PROMPT

Social Studies

American Indians and colonists used land for different purposes than the way it is used today.

- What is one way the colonists used the land that differs from the way the American Indians used it?
- How is land used differently today?

JOURNAL PROMPT

Social Studies

In Social Studies we read about Native Americans using their environment for survival.

- What environmental features were used by Native Americans?
- Do people today use the same features? How?
- What questions do you have about this topic?

JOURNAL PROMPT

Social Studies

The first Americans are believed to have come across the land bridge from Asia.

- Describe the land bridge.
- Do you think this could ever happen again? Why?

JOURNAL PROMPT

Social Studies

Everyone has ancestors.

- What are ancestors?
- Do you think it is important to know about your ancestors? Why or why not?

JOURNAL PROMPT

Social Studies

During the Revolutionary War the patriots and loyalists had completely different views.

- Compare and contrast the patriots and the loyalists.
- Explain which group you would have sided with.
- How does the outcome of this war affect you today?

JOURNAL PROMPT

Social Studies

During the Revolutionary War the English soldiers were often called Redcoats.

- Why were they called this?
- Compare the English military with the minutemen.
- Compare the minutemen with our military today.
- How does our military today affect your life?

JOURNAL PROMPT

Social Studies

The Revolutionary War was fought between England and the colonists. The colonists won the war.

- Why is it important to know this information?
- What would have been different today if England had won the war?
- Do you think your life might be different? In what way?

JOURNAL PROMPT

Social Studies

During the Civil War the North and the South had different views about the war.

- Compare and contrast the views of the North and the South.
- Who do you agree with most and why?
- How did the Civil War affect your life today?

JOURNAL PROMPT

Social Studies

We have been reading about the Civil War between the North and the South. The North won the war.

- What advantages did the North have?
- What disadvantages did they face?
- Why is it important for you to know about the Civil War?

JOURNAL PROMPT

Social Studies

In Social Studies we read about historical things that have happened before we were alive.

- Do you think it is important to understand what happened before you were alive? Why?
- What event in United States history do you think affects you most today? Why?

JOURNAL PROMPT

Social Studies

Before the Civil War slaves used the Underground Railroad to escape to freedom. Code words were used. Circle one of these code words:

trains   *conductor*   *stations*

- What does this word mean when talking about the Underground Railroad?
- Why do you think code words were used?

JOURNAL PROMPT

Social Studies

Every country has features that make it unique, beautiful, and interesting.

- Choose a country that you have been reading about and describe it. Use the reading material to find words that describe this country.
- Would you like to visit this country? Why or why not?

Journal Prompt

Social Studies

Productive services (human resources and natural resources) and capital resources are used in your community to produce goods and services.

- Choose one type of productive service and give an example of this in your community.
- How does this affect you?

Journal Prompt

Social Studies

Sometimes people trade for something rather than pay for it.

- When might someone do this?
- Has this ever happened to you? Explain your answer.

JOURNAL PROMPT

Social Studies

Suppose you went shopping for shoes with your mother.

- How would you decide which shoes to buy?
- Would your mother have the same reasons for deciding which shoes to buy? Explain your answer.

JOURNAL PROMPT

Social Studies

Everyone lives in some type of community.

- How is your community like most others?
- How is your community different from others?
- What do you like most about your community?

SCIENCE

Writing in response to reading should take place in all subject areas. In Science students can respond using the same skills mentioned in Literary Response. Students are responding to informative or expository text.

JOURNAL PROMPT

Science

Plants and animals have external features that help them live in different environments. Choose one plant or animal that the class has been discussing.

- Describe the external features of the plant or animal.
- How do these external features help the plant or animal survive in its environment?

JOURNAL PROMPT

Science

Place the following living things into groups according to features they share. Label each group.

tigers   children   whales   men

lions   starfish   zebras

women   elephants   lobsters

Explain the features you used to sort these living things into groups.

Sonia Tuttle - Journal Bites- 2009

JOURNAL PROMPT

Science

People are more like other people than they are like other animals.

- In what ways are you like other people?
- Do other animals have these same features?

JOURNAL PROMPT

Science

Some environments, such as deserts or the arctic, have extreme features and temperatures. Think about where you live.

- What features are present in your environment?
- How do these features compare to living in an extreme environment?

JOURNAL PROMPT

Science

You probably look like either your mother or father, or maybe you have characteristics of both.

- In what ways do you resemble your parents?
- What causes this to happen?

JOURNAL PROMPT

Science

The class has been reading about volcanoes and earthquakes.

- Describe volcanoes.
- Describe earthquakes.
- Would either of these affect you where you live? Explain your answer.

Journal Prompt

Science

You have been reading about volcanoes.

- Could your life be affected by a volcano? Why?
- Do you think it is important to know about volcanoes? Explain your answer.

Journal Prompt

Science

As a child you received vaccinations for some diseases.

- What is one disease that you can get a vaccination for?
- Why is this important?
- Predict what would happen if people stopped getting vaccines.

JOURNAL PROMPT

Science

People can spread germs to other people, causing diseases.

- What is one disease you can get from germs spread by another person?
- What is one way you can keep this from happening?

JOURNAL PROMPT

Science

Sometimes when we change one thing, it causes other changes to take place. An example of this is, when we exercise, there is an effect on our heart rate.

- What is another way you could cause a change in your body?
- Describe the effect this would have on your body.
- Would this be a positive or negative effect? Explain.

JOURNAL PROMPT

Science

As you grow, your body changes.

- How does your need for exercise change as you grow?
- Why do you think this happens?

JOURNAL PROMPT

Science

Human beings have body systems.

- What body systems do you have?
- Choose one body system and describe it.
- Tell why this system is important to your body.

JOURNAL PROMPT

Science

In the space below, draw an organizer to compare and contrast two body systems. Then write a paragraph comparing the two.

JOURNAL PROMPT

Science

Getting enough rest can help you stay healthy.

- How much rest do you get each night during the week?
- Do you think this is enough rest to help you stay healthy? Why or why not?

JOURNAL PROMPT

Science

Vitamins and minerals can be found in many foods that we eat.

- Why is it important to eat foods that contain vitamins and minerals?
- Make a list of some of these foods.

JOURNAL PROMPT

Science

Eating a variety of healthful foods can keep you healthy.

- Describe a healthful food that you like to eat.
- How will eating this food help keep you healthy?

JOURNAL PROMPT

Science

You have been reading about the dangers of drugs.

- How important is this information to you? Why?
- Do you think cigarettes could be considered a drug? Explain your answer.
- How do cigarettes and drugs affect your life?

JOURNAL PROMPT

Science

Constellations can be seen in the night sky.

- What are constellations?
- What are some constellations that you know?
- How have constellations been used by people over the years?

Journal Prompt

Science

In the summer, the sun is hotter and the days are longer.

- What causes this?
- What effects does this have on the earth?
- What effects does this have on your life?

Journal Prompt

Science

In space there is no gravity.

- What would be different on Earth if there was no gravity?
- When could this be a good thing?
- When might this be a bad thing?

JOURNAL PROMPT

Science

List the following food groups in order of importance in your diet.

fruits and vegetables   *dairy*
fats   *grains*   *meat(protein)*

- Explain why you chose this order.

JOURNAL PROMPT

Science

Technology has greatly changed our lives.

- How has the invention of computers changed your life?
- How does the invention of new medicines change lives?
- Why do you think the benefits of computers and medicine have not affected the lives of everyone?